MASTERING YOUR DENTAL PRACTICE

A COMPREHENSIVE GUIDE TO SELF-GRADING YOUR ONLINE AND DIGITAL MARKETING

By

Rivers Morrell CEO / Founder of Gumline Marketing & Jeff Jones President / Founder of Gumline Marketing.

Rivers Morrell, a seasoned marketing veteran with over two decades of online marketing experience, is a distinguished authority in dental marketing. He is the CEO and founder of Gumline Marketing, a dental marketing company. As the accomplished author of "Mastering Your Dental Practice: A Comprehensive Guide to Self-Grading Your Online and Digital Marketing," Rivers brings forth a wealth of knowledge and insights from his extensive journey in dental and healthcare marketing. Rivers lives in Knoxville with his wife and two children. He loves the outdoors, swimming, the beach and traveling with his family

Jeff Jones has over 2 decades of experience in online customer acquisition with a special focus on dental and healthcare. He is the President and founder of Gumline Marketing.

Contents

Background _____ 5

Unleashing the Power of Your Digital Showcase: A Comprehensive Guide to Crafting a Captivating Dental Website _____ 11

Mastering Local SEO: Your Blueprint to Dominating the Digital Landscape Locally _____ 18

Mastering Precision: A Comprehensive Guide to Unlocking the Power of PPC Advertising in Dental Marketing _____ 24

Crafting a Dynamic Social Media Presence: A Comprehensive Guide for Dental Practices _____ 30

Mastering the Art of Email Marketing: A Comprehensive Guide for Dental Practices _____ 35

Unleashing the Potential of Video Marketing: A Comprehensive Guide for Dental Practices _____ 41

Mastering Dental SEO: A Strategic Guide to Amplify Your Online Presence _____ 46

Revolutionizing Patient Experience: A Comprehensive Guide to Implementing Online Appointment Scheduling _____ 51

Elevating Your Dental Practice: The Power of Engaging Social Media Contests. _____ 56

Mastering Dental Marketing: The Art of Educational Webinars and Workshops _____ 61

Navigating the Realm of Dental Marketing: A Comprehensive Guide to Influencer Marketing _____ 66

Navigating the Mobile Revolution: A Comprehensive Guide to Optimizing Your Dental Marketing for Mobile Platforms _____ 71

Crafting Personalized Patient Journeys: A Comprehensive Guide to Optimizing Dental Marketing through Targeted Landing Pages _____ 77

Crafting a Comprehensive Patient Education Hub: Elevating Your Practice as an Authority in Oral Health _____ 83

Elevating Your Dental Marketing: A Comprehensive Guide to Mastering Google Ads Remarketing _____ 88

Mastering Voice Search Optimization: Navigating the Future of Dental Marketing_____ 94

Building Community Connections: A Guide to Strengthening Your Dental Practice Through Local Collaborations _____ 100

Mastering Social Media Retargeting: A Comprehensive Guide for Dental Practices_____ 105

Elevating Your Dental Marketing Strategy: A Guide to Data-Driven Excellence_____ 109

BACKGROUND

Welcome, esteemed dentists and dental office managers, to a journey into the realm of online and digital marketing. In this guide, we will explore the critical strategies that can revolutionize your approach to attracting new patients. As a dental marketing company, we understand the unique challenges you face in promoting your practice. Today, we're not just offering insights; we're empowering you to self-grade and enhance your online and digital marketing efforts. Let's dive into the world of dental marketing mastery with "20 Online and Digital Marketing Strategies to Get New Patients for Your Dental Practice."

1. Crafting a Captivating Website: The Digital Showcase of Your Practice

Your website is the cornerstone of your online presence. Evaluate its visual appeal, ease of navigation, and mobile responsiveness. Ensure it reflects the professionalism and warmth of your physical clinic. A compelling website invites patients into your digital space, setting the stage for a positive online experience.

2. Mastering Local SEO: Be Found Where It Matters

Optimize your website for local search engine optimization (SEO). Claim your Google My Business listing, use local keywords, and encourage satisfied patients to leave positive reviews. Local SEO ensures your practice is visible to those actively seeking dental services in your area.

3. Unlocking the Power of PPC Advertising: Precision in Patient Targeting

Dive into the world of Pay-Per-Click (PPC) advertising. Strategically choose keywords, create compelling ad copy, and leverage targeted campaigns. PPC ensures your practice appears at the forefront when potential patients are actively searching for dental services, delivering a remarkable return on investment.

4. Building a Social Media Presence: Connect Beyond the Clinic Walls

Harness the vast reach of social media platforms. Establish a consistent presence on channels like Facebook, Instagram, and Twitter. Engage with your audience through informative content, patient stories, and promotions. Social media serves as a dynamic extension of your practice, fostering connections beyond the clinic.

5. Embracing Email Marketing: Nurturing Relationships Digitally

Develop a robust email marketing strategy. Regular newsletters, promotions, and educational content keep your practice top of mind. Email marketing nurtures relationships, encouraging patient loyalty and retention.

6. Leveraging the Power of Video Marketing: A Personal Touch in the Digital Realm

Engage your audience with video marketing. Share behind-the-scenes glimpses of your practice, educational content, and patient testimonials. Video adds a personal touch, making your practice more relatable and trustworthy.

7. Prioritizing Dental SEO: Elevate Your Online Visibility

Invest in comprehensive Search Engine Optimization (SEO) for your dental website. Optimize content, meta tags, and images. Quality backlinks enhance your website's authority, ensuring your practice ranks higher in search engine results.

8. Implementing Online Appointment Scheduling: Convenience at Your Patient's Fingertips

Enhance patient experience with online appointment scheduling. Simplify the booking process, saving time for both your team and patients. The convenience of online scheduling encourages prompt bookings.

9. Engaging Social Media Contests: Gamify Your Online Presence

Boost engagement with social media contests. Encourage participation through likes, shares, and comments. Contests not only entertain your audience but also broaden your social media reach.

10. Educational Webinars and Workshops: Positioning as an Industry Expert

Share your expertise through webinars and online workshops. Cover topics ranging from oral health tips to the latest advancements in dentistry. Positioning yourself as an industry expert enhances your practice's credibility.

11. Influencer Marketing: Collaboration for Authenticity

Collaborate with influencers in the dental and healthcare space. Their endorsements bring authenticity to your practice and resonate with their followers. Influencer marketing can significantly expand your online reach.

12. Optimizing for Mobile Platforms: Meeting Patients Where They Are

Recognize the prevalence of mobile device usage. Optimize your online content for mobile platforms. Responsive design, SMS marketing, and mobile-friendly content ensure accessibility for your mobile audience.

13. Creating Targeted Landing Pages: Personalized Patient Journeys

Develop targeted landing pages for specific services or promotions. Personalize your message to specific audience segments. A tailored approach increases the likelihood of patient conversion.

14. Providing Valuable Online Patient Education: A Hub for Oral Health Knowledge

Become a go-to resource for oral health information. Share informative blog posts, articles, and downloadable guides. Educational content not only informs your audience but also positions your practice as a trusted authority.

15. Implementing Google Ads Remarketing: Stay on Your Patient's Mind

Reconnect with users who have previously visited your website through Google Ads remarketing campaigns. This subtle reminder often prompts them to revisit and schedule appointments.

16. Optimizing for Voice Search: Anticipating Future Search Trends

Prepare for the rise of voice-activated devices. Optimize your online content for voice search. Using conversational keywords and providing concise, informative answers makes your practice more accessible.

17. Collaborating with Local Businesses: Strengthening Community Connections

Build partnerships with other local businesses. Cross-promotions and shared initiatives not only expand your reach but also strengthen community ties. A collaborative approach benefits both your practice and the local ecosystem.

18. Implementing Retargeting Ads on Social Media: Staying in Your Patient's Feed

Utilize retargeting ads on platforms like Facebook and Instagram. Keep your practice visible to users who have shown interest. Retargeting ads serve as gentle reminders and encourage users to take the next step.

19. Continuous Monitoring and Adaptation: Data-Driven Decision Making

Regularly analyze data from website analytics, social media insights, and advertising platforms. Adapt your strategies based on performance metrics. Data-driven decision-making ensures continuous improvement and sustained growth.

CHAPTER 1

UNLEASHING THE POWER OF YOUR DIGITAL SHOWCASE: A COMPREHENSIVE GUIDE TO CRAFTING A CAPTIVATING DENTAL WEBSITE

Understanding the Significance of Your Digital Showcase

Your website is the cornerstone of your online presence, acting as the digital face of your dental practice. It's where potential patients gain their first impression of your clinic, its services, and the experience they can expect. Just as you meticulously design the physical layout of your practice for optimal patient comfort, your website should be a seamless extension that reflects the same professionalism, warmth, and commitment to exceptional patient care.

Evaluating Visual Appeal: Painting a Picture of Excellence

Harmonizing Branding Elements:

Begin by evaluating the visual appeal of your website. Consistency in branding elements—such as your logo, color palette, and imagery—is key. Assess whether these elements create a cohesive and visually pleasing representation of your practice. A harmonious blend reinforces your brand identity and leaves a lasting impression.

Image Quality and Authenticity:

Next, scrutinize the quality and authenticity of the images featured on your website. High-resolution, genuine images of your team, facilities, and satisfied patients contribute to the visual narrative of your practice. Authenticity builds trust and creates an inviting atmosphere for potential patients exploring your digital space.

Color Psychology:

Consider the color psychology employed in your website design. Colors evoke emotions and perceptions. Reflect on whether your chosen color palette aligns with the desired ambiance of your practice. Thoughtful color selection can enhance the overall user experience and reinforce your brand personality.

Navigational Simplicity: Guiding Users with Intuition

Intuitive Menu Structure:

Moving beyond visual appeal, assess the ease of navigation. Your website should be user-friendly, with an intuitive menu structure that guides visitors effortlessly. Logical grouping of related pages ensures that users can quickly locate the information they are seeking. A seamless navigation experience reflects positively on your practice's organizational competence.

Strategic Call-to-Action (CTA):

Examine the placement and clarity of Call-to-Action (CTA) buttons on your website. Strategic positioning of CTAs, whether for appointment scheduling, contact information, or service exploration, ensures that visitors are guided towards meaningful actions. The path from interest to action should be clear, reducing friction for potential patients.

Search Functionality:

Consider the effectiveness of the search functionality on your website. A functional search bar aids users in finding specific information promptly. For those who prefer a direct approach, an efficient search feature enhances user convenience and ensures a positive overall experience.

Mobile Responsiveness: Adapting to the Mobile-First Era

Responsive Design:

In the era dominated by mobile devices, optimizing your website for mobile responsiveness is no longer an option—it's a necessity. Evaluate the responsiveness of your website across various devices. Responsive design ensures a consistent and user-friendly experience on smartphones, tablets, and other devices with varying screen sizes.

Loading Speed:

Assess the loading speed of your website, paying special attention to mobile devices. Mobile users, in particular, appreciate a website that loads swiftly. Optimize images and minimize unnecessary elements to ensure a seamless experience, even on slower mobile connections.

Touch-Friendly Elements:

Design touch-friendly buttons and interactive elements for mobile users. With touch gestures being a primary mode of interaction on mobile devices, ensuring a smooth and intuitive touch experience enhances overall satisfaction. Users should be able to navigate your website effortlessly using touch gestures.

Ensuring Professionalism and Trust: Elements of Credibility

Testimonials and Reviews:

Building trust is paramount. Showcase patient testimonials and reviews prominently on your website. Authentic feedback from satisfied patients serves as a powerful endorsement of your practice. Consider implementing a system for collecting and featuring ongoing testimonials to keep your digital showcase dynamic.

Credentials Display:

Highlight the credentials and certifications of your team members. Ensure that this information is displayed prominently on relevant pages. Transparently showcasing the qualifications of your dental professionals reinforces your practice's expertise and professionalism.

Transparent Information:

Evaluate the transparency of information provided on your website. Clear and comprehensive details about your practice, services, and policies minimize uncertainty for potential patients. A transparent approach fosters trust and helps patients make informed decisions.

Crafting a User-Centric Experience: Encouraging Exploration

Clear Service Descriptions:

The presentation of your dental services is a critical component. Provide clear and concise descriptions of each service offered. Break down complex dental procedures into understandable terms for patients. A well-articulated description enhances the accessibility of your services.

Visual Aids Integration:

Enhance service pages with visual aids, such as infographics or videos. Visual representations make information more digestible and engaging. Consider incorporating multimedia elements that showcase your practice's commitment to patient education and satisfaction.

FAQ Inclusion:

Anticipate patient queries by including a comprehensive Frequently Asked Questions (FAQ) section. Addressing common questions proactively demonstrates your commitment to patient education. A well-structured FAQ section can significantly enhance the user experience.

The Journey Continues: Continuous Optimization

Your journey to crafting a captivating website doesn't end with its initial creation. Website optimization is an ongoing commitment to excellence. Regularly revisit and adapt your website to align with evolving patient expectations, technological advancements, and industry trends.

Continuous Optimization Strategies:

- Content Updates: Keep your website content fresh by updating it regularly. This not only benefits your Search Engine Optimization (SEO) efforts but also demonstrates your commitment to providing current and relevant information.

- Performance Monitoring: Utilize analytics tools to monitor website performance. Track user behavior, page views, and conversion rates to identify areas for improvement. Analyzing these metrics ensures that your website remains aligned with user preferences.

- Security Measures: Prioritize website security to protect patient information. Regularly update software, use secure hosting, and implement encryption protocols. Ensuring the security of your digital showcase builds trust with potential patients.

CHAPTER 2

MASTERING LOCAL SEO: YOUR BLUEPRINT TO DOMINATING THE DIGITAL LANDSCAPE LOCALLY

The Local SEO Advantage: An In-Depth Exploration

Before we dive into the intricacies, let's lay the groundwork by understanding the profound impact of Local SEO on your dental practice. In an era dominated by digital searches, the ability to be found by potential patients in your local vicinity is a game-changer. Local SEO is the secret sauce that elevates your practice's visibility, making it discoverable by those actively seeking dental services in your geographical area.

Claim Your Digital Identity - Google My Business (GMB) Optimization

Claim and Verify Your GMB Listing

The journey begins with your Google My Business (GMB) listing, the digital gateway to your practice. If you haven't already, claim and verify your GMB listing. This is not just a procedural step; it's the foundation on which your local digital presence is built.

Complete Your GMB Profile

Once claimed, dive into the details. Complete every facet of your GMB profile with meticulous care. Accurate business information, operating hours, contact details, and a compelling business description are not mere data points—they are critical elements that contribute to your local search visibility.

Add High-Quality Visuals

A picture is worth a thousand words, especially in the digital landscape. Populate your GMB profile with high-quality images of your dental practice, your team, and the welcoming ambiance within. Visual storytelling adds a personal touch, creating a connection with potential patients.

Encourage Reviews on GMB

Patient reviews on your GMB listing are powerful testimonials. Actively encourage satisfied patients to leave positive reviews. Respond to reviews, positive or otherwise, with professionalism. Positive reviews enhance your online reputation, while addressing criticism demonstrates your commitment to patient satisfaction.

Harnessing the Power of Local Keywords

Conduct Local Keyword Research

Local keywords are the compass guiding potential patients to your digital doorstep. Utilize tools like Google Keyword Planner to understand the language of your local audience. Uncover the terms they commonly use when seeking dental services in your area.

Optimize On-Page Content

With your local keyword arsenal in hand, strategically infuse these terms into your website's on-page content. From your homepage to service pages, ensure that your content is not just informative but also aligns seamlessly with the local keywords your audience is using.

Localized Meta Tags and Descriptions

Fine-tune your meta tags and descriptions with a local flair. These snippets are the first glimpse potential patients get on search engine result pages. Craft them to be captivating, informative, and locally relevant. A compelling meta tag can be the difference between a click and a scroll.

Building a Robust Local Link Ecosystem

Cultivate Local Backlinks

Backlinks from local sources amplify your local SEO strength. Cultivate relationships with local businesses, chambers of commerce, or community organizations. Seek opportunities for collaborations or sponsorships that can organically lead to credible backlinks.

Local Directories and Citations

Ensure your practice is accurately listed in local directories and citation sources. Consistency in your business name, address, and phone number (NAP) across various platforms is not just a best practice; it's a foundational element that Google values when determining local search rankings.

The Mobile Revolution: Local SEO's Best Friend

Optimize for Mobile Devices

The mobile revolution is in full swing, and your website must be at the forefront. Ensure that your website is not just mobile-friendly but optimized for a stellar mobile experience. Google prioritizes mobile-friendly websites, and so should you.

Voice Search Optimization

Voice-activated devices are changing the search landscape. Understand how people in your area phrase voice queries related to dental services. Optimize your content to align with these conversational search patterns, ensuring that your practice is voice-search ready.

Analytics and Continuous Improvement

Set Up Google Analytics and Search Console

To measure the effectiveness of your local SEO efforts, set up Google Analytics and Google Search Console. These tools provide invaluable insights into website traffic, user behavior, and search performance. Regularly analyze the data to identify areas for improvement.

Local SEO Audits

Conduct regular local SEO audits to assess the effectiveness of your strategies. Evaluate your GMB listing, keyword performance, backlink profile, and overall website health. Address any issues promptly to maintain and enhance your local search visibility.

Local SEO in Action - A Case Study

To exemplify the transformative power of local SEO, let's delve into a hypothetical case study. Dr. Smith, a dentist in [Your City], implemented a comprehensive local SEO strategy. Over a six-month period, the practice experienced:

- A 50% Increase in GMB Impressions: Dr. Smith's optimized GMB listing reached more potential patients, making a significant impact on local visibility.

- A 25% Rise in Positive Reviews: Actively encouraging reviews resulted in a 25% increase in positive feedback, fortifying the practice's online reputation.

- A 30% Growth in Local Organic Traffic: Local keyword optimization and backlink building contributed to a substantial increase in organic traffic from local searches, putting Dr. Smith's practice on the digital map.

CHAPTER 3

MASTERING PRECISION: A COMPREHENSIVE GUIDE TO UNLOCKING THE POWER OF PPC ADVERTISING IN DENTAL MARKETING

As your trusted dental marketing companion, we embark on a coaching journey to empower you with the knowledge and strategies needed to grade and elevate your own PPC advertising efforts. Join us as we delve into the intricacies of strategically choosing keywords, crafting compelling ad copy, and unleashing the potential of targeted campaigns. By the end of this comprehensive guide, you'll not only understand the nuances of PPC advertising but also possess the tools to assess and refine your own strategies.

The Essence of PPC Advertising

The Foundation - What is PPC?

At its core, PPC advertising is a digital marketing strategy where advertisers pay a fee each time their ad is clicked. It's a dynamic and results-driven approach that places your dental practice at the forefront when potential patients actively search for dental services. The essence lies in paying for the visibility that directly aligns with patient intent.

The Power of Precision

The magic happens in precision. PPC allows you to strategically target your audience based on keywords, demographics, location, and even the device they are using. Precision in patient targeting ensures that your investment is directed towards those actively seeking dental services, maximizing the chances of conversion.

Strategically Choosing Keywords

The Keyword Research Ballet

The dance begins with meticulous keyword research. Identify the terms potential patients are using when searching for dental services. Tools like Google Keyword Planner and competitor analysis can unveil the language your audience speaks. Build a robust keyword list that forms the foundation of your PPC campaign.

Long-Tail Keywords - Your Secret Weapon

While generic keywords have their place, don't underestimate the power of long-tail keywords. These are more specific phrases that capture the nuances of what patients are looking for. Long-tail keywords may have lower search volumes, but they often lead to higher conversion rates.

Negative Keywords - Sculpting Precision

Just as important as choosing the right keywords is excluding the wrong ones. Negative keywords ensure your ads don't appear for irrelevant searches, refining your targeting and maximizing your budget.

Crafting Compelling Ad Copy

The Art of Captivating Headlines

Your headline is the first impression. Craft headlines that are not just informative but also attention-grabbing. A well-crafted headline sparks curiosity and entices potential patients to delve deeper.

Persuasive Ad Descriptions

The body of your ad is where persuasion takes center stage. Clearly communicate the unique value propositions of your dental practice. Address patient pain points, highlight services, and include a compelling call-to-action that encourages clicks.

Utilizing Ad Extensions

Ad extensions are the secret sauce to enhance your ad's visibility and provide additional information. Whether it's site links, callouts, or structured snippets, ad extensions amplify the value of your ad, offering potential patients more reasons to choose your practice.

Leveraging Targeted Campaigns

Geo-Targeting - Bringing Patients Closer

Geo-targeting allows you to show your ads to potential patients based on their location. For a dental practice, this means ensuring your ads are visible to those in your immediate service area. Precision in location targeting eliminates wasteful clicks from irrelevant regions.

Device Targeting - Adapting to User Habits

Understand the devices your potential patients use. Mobile devices, tablets, and desktops each have unique user behaviors. Tailor your campaigns to these habits, optimizing the user experience and maximizing the impact of your PPC efforts.

Dayparting - Timing is Everything

Timing can be the difference between a click and a missed opportunity. Dayparting allows you to schedule your ads to appear at specific times of the day or days of the week.

Consider when your potential patients are most likely to search and interact with your ads.

The Remarkable ROI of PPC Advertising

Measuring Success - Key Metrics to Monitor

To grade your PPC efforts, you need to know what success looks like. Monitor key metrics such as Click-Through Rate (CTR), Conversion Rate, Cost Per Click (CPC), and Return on Ad Spend (ROAS). These metrics provide insights into the effectiveness of your campaigns.

Continuous Optimization - A Dynamic Process

The beauty of PPC is its adaptability. Continuous optimization is not just a best practice; it's a necessity. Regularly review and refine your keyword list, ad copy, and targeting parameters. Stay agile in response to shifting patient behaviors and market dynamics.

PPC in Action - A Case Study

Realizing Success Metrics

To illustrate the transformative power of PPC advertising, let's delve into a hypothetical case study. Dr. Anderson, a dentist in [Your City], implemented a targeted PPC campaign. Over a three-month period, the practice experienced:

- A 30% Increase in Click-Through Rate (CTR): Dr. Anderson's ads were more compelling and resonated with potential patients, leading to a significant increase in clicks.

- A 20% Decrease in Cost Per Click (CPC): Optimization efforts resulted in a more efficient use of budget, lowering the cost per click while maintaining visibility.

- A 40% Boost in Conversion Rate: The precision in targeting led to a higher conversion rate, converting more clicks into actual patients.

CHAPTER 4

CRAFTING A DYNAMIC SOCIAL MEDIA PRESENCE: A COMPREHENSIVE GUIDE FOR DENTAL PRACTICES

Defining Your Social Media Presence

Your social media presence is more than just a collection of posts; it's a digital reflection of your practice's personality. Define the tone, style, and objectives of your social media journey. Are you aiming for a professional tone, a friendly vibe, or a blend of both? Clearly outlining your social media identity sets the foundation for a cohesive and engaging online presence.

Understanding the Social Landscape

Each social media platform has its unique characteristics and user demographics. Understand the nuances of platforms like Facebook, Instagram, and Twitter. Tailor your content to align with the preferences of each audience. Facebook may be ideal for longer-form content, while Instagram thrives on visual storytelling. Twitter, with its concise nature, caters to real-time engagement.

Establishing a Consistent Presence

Content Calendar Mastery

Consistency is key in the realm of social media. Craft a content calendar outlining the frequency and types of posts. Consider thematic days, such as "Wellness Wednesday" or "Smile Saturday," to infuse variety and engage your audience regularly. A well-structured content calendar ensures a steady flow of engaging content.

Visual Brilliance

Visual appeal is the heart of social media. Invest in high-quality visuals that resonate with your brand. Showcase your dental practice through captivating images of the clinic, your team, and happy patients. Strive for a cohesive visual identity across all platforms to strengthen brand recognition.

Audience Engagement Strategies

Informative Content Sharing

Educate and empower your audience through informative content. Share oral health tips, industry insights, and relevant news. Establish your practice as a knowledgeable resource, fostering trust and positioning yourself as an authority in dental care.

Patient Stories and Testimonials

Humanize your practice by sharing patient stories and testimonials. With their consent, feature before-and-after photos, success stories, and testimonials. This not only adds a personal touch but also showcases the positive impact of your dental care services.

Promotions and Specials

Inject excitement into your social media presence by occasionally featuring promotions and specials. Whether it's a teeth-whitening offer, a referral program, or a seasonal discount, promotions encourage engagement and motivate your audience to take action.

Social Media as a Dynamic Extension

Real-Time Engagement

Social media is a real-time platform. Respond promptly to comments, messages, and mentions. Foster two-way communication by actively engaging with your audience. Whether it's answering queries, thanking patients for positive feedback, or addressing concerns, real-time engagement builds a sense of community.

Live Video and Stories

Embrace the dynamic nature of live video and stories. Host Q&A sessions, behind-the-scenes glimpses, or live dental education sessions. Stories, with their ephemeral nature, create a sense of urgency, encouraging your audience to tune in regularly for fresh content.

Community Building

Beyond promotional content, focus on community building. Create polls, ask questions, and encourage your audience to share their experiences. By fostering a sense of community, your social media becomes more than a marketing tool; it becomes a space where patients connect with each other and with your practice.

Measuring Social Media Success

Key Metrics for Evaluation

To grade your social media efforts, understand and monitor key metrics. Track engagement metrics such as likes, shares, comments, and click-through rates. Analyze follower growth, post reach, and audience demographics to gain insights into your social media performance.

Social Listening Tools

Utilize social listening tools to understand what patients are saying about your practice and the industry. Monitor conversations, track brand mentions, and identify opportunities for improvement. Social listening provides valuable feedback for refining your social media strategy.

Social Media in Action - A Case Study

Transformative Success Metrics

Let's explore a hypothetical case study to illustrate the transformative impact of a well-executed social media strategy:

- Increased Engagement by 40%: Regular, engaging content resonated with the audience, leading to a substantial increase in likes, shares, and comments.

- Positive Sentiment Growth: Social listening tools revealed a surge in positive sentiment, indicating improved brand perception within the community.

- New Patient Acquisitions: Strategic promotions and community building efforts translated into a notable increase in new patient acquisitions.

CHAPTER 5

MASTERING THE ART OF EMAIL MARKETING: A COMPREHENSIVE GUIDE FOR DENTAL PRACTICES

Unveiling the Potential of Email

Email marketing is not just about sending messages; it's a dynamic tool to connect with your audience. It goes beyond the clinic walls, allowing you to foster relationships, communicate valuable information, and solidify your practice's presence in the digital landscape.

Understanding Patient Engagement

Patient engagement is at the heart of successful email marketing. It's not just about delivering messages but creating content that resonates. Understanding patient behaviors, preferences, and expectations forms the foundation for a robust email marketing strategy.

Developing a Robust Email Marketing Strategy

Building Your Email List

Your email list is the lifeline of your email marketing efforts. Strategically build and segment your list based on patient demographics, preferences, and engagement levels. A well-organized email list lays the groundwork for targeted and personalized communication.

Crafting Compelling Content

Compelling content is the driving force behind successful email marketing. From regular newsletters that keep patients informed to promotions that spark excitement, every email should deliver value. Incorporate educational content, service highlights, and patient stories to create a well-rounded email strategy.

Personalization and Segmentation

Personalization adds a human touch to your emails. Leverage patient data to personalize messages, addressing recipients by name and tailoring content based on their history with your practice. Segmentation further refines targeting, ensuring that each email resonates with its intended audience.

Regular Newsletters - A Cornerstone of Communication

Establishing a Newsletter Calendar

Consistency is paramount in newsletter communication. Develop a calendar outlining the frequency and themes of your newsletters. Whether it's a monthly recap, seasonal promotions, or oral health tips, a well-structured calendar ensures a steady flow of engaging content.

Informative Updates and News

Newsletters serve as a platform for informative updates. Share practice news, introduce team members, and highlight achievements. Keep patients informed about changes, innovations, and any relevant developments within your practice.

Educational Content

Educate and empower your patients through educational content. From oral health tips and preventive care advice to information about new dental technologies, educational content positions your practice as a valuable resource.

Promotions and Special Offers

Creating Irresistible Promotions

Promotions add an element of excitement to your email marketing strategy. Craft promotions that capture attention, whether it's a discount on teeth whitening, a referral program, or a seasonal offer. Promotions encourage patient engagement and drive action.

Exclusive Patient Offers

Reward patient loyalty through exclusive offers. Create campaigns that provide special discounts, early access to promotions, or loyalty programs for long-time patients. Exclusive offers enhance the sense of belonging and appreciation among your patient community.

Encouraging Patient Loyalty and Retention

Personalized Follow-Ups

Follow-up emails based on patient interactions foster a personalized connection. Send thank-you emails after appointments, follow up on treatment plans, and celebrate patient milestones. Personalized follow-ups demonstrate genuine care and strengthen patient loyalty.

Patient Appreciation Campaigns

Showcase your appreciation for your patients through dedicated campaigns. Celebrate patient birthdays, anniversaries with the practice, or other special occasions. Thoughtful gestures foster a sense of belonging and contribute to long-term patient retention.

Gathering Patient Feedback

Emails serve as an effective tool for gathering patient feedback. Send surveys or feedback forms to understand patient experiences and expectations. Act on the feedback received to continuously improve and adapt your services.

Measuring Email Marketing Success

Key Metrics for Evaluation

To grade your email marketing efforts, understand and monitor key metrics. Track metrics such as open rates, click-through rates, conversion rates, and unsubscribe rates. These metrics provide insights into the effectiveness of your campaigns.

A/B Testing Strategies

Experiment with A/B testing to refine your email marketing strategy. Test different subject lines, content formats, and calls-to-action to understand what resonates most with your audience. A/B testing enables continuous optimization for better results.

Email Marketing in Action - A Case Study

Transformative Success Metrics

Let's delve into a hypothetical case study to illustrate the transformative impact of a well-executed email marketing strategy:

- Increased Open Rates by 20%: Strategic content and personalization led to a significant increase in email open rates, indicating heightened patient engagement.

- Enhanced Patient Retention: Targeted follow-up emails and patient appreciation campaigns contributed to a notable improvement in patient retention rates.

- Successful Promotion Conversion: A carefully crafted promotion resulted in a high conversion rate, driving patient action and participation.

CHAPTER 6

UNLEASHING THE POTENTIAL OF VIDEO MARKETING: A COMPREHENSIVE GUIDE FOR DENTAL PRACTICES

Embracing the Visual Revolution

In an era dominated by visual content, video marketing stands out as a powerful medium for storytelling. It transcends traditional marketing methods, allowing your practice to convey messages, showcase expertise, and build connections in ways that text and static images cannot.

Understanding the Impact of Video

Video is more than a visual feast for your audience; it's an immersive experience. Understand the impact of video on viewer engagement, brand perception, and conversion rates. Video marketing has the potential to create a lasting impression, driving patient trust and loyalty.

Types of Videos for Dental Practices

Behind-the-Scenes Glimpses

Invite your audience into the heart of your practice with behind-the-scenes glimpses. Showcase your team, state-of-the-art equipment, and the welcoming atmosphere of your clinic. Humanize your practice, allowing patients to connect with the people who make their dental experiences exceptional.

Educational Content

Educate and empower your audience with informative videos. From oral health tips and procedural walkthroughs to discussions about the latest dental technologies, educational content positions your practice as an authority in dental care. Use video to demystify procedures and instill confidence in your patients.

Patient Testimonials

Let your satisfied patients share their stories through video testimonials. Authentic testimonials build trust and provide potential patients with insights into the positive experiences others have had with your practice. Patient testimonials add a personal touch that resonates deeply with viewers.

The Art of Crafting Compelling Videos

Planning Your Video Content

Before hitting record, meticulously plan your video content. Identify your target audience, set clear objectives, and outline the key messages you want to convey. A well-thought-out plan ensures that your videos align with your practice's overall marketing strategy.

Embracing Authenticity

Authenticity is the cornerstone of effective video marketing. Be genuine, transparent, and true to your practice's identity. Viewers connect with authenticity, making your videos more relatable and establishing a foundation of trust.

Capturing Quality Footage

Invest in quality equipment to capture crisp and professional footage. While smartphones can produce impressive videos, consider using a dedicated camera for higher production quality. Pay attention to lighting, audio, and framing to ensure your videos are visually appealing and easy to follow.

Platforms and Distribution Strategies

Leveraging YouTube

YouTube is a powerhouse for video content. Create a dedicated channel for your practice, organizing videos into playlists for easy navigation. Optimize video titles, descriptions, and tags to enhance discoverability. YouTube serves as a comprehensive video repository for your practice's digital presence.

Social Media Integration

Integrate videos seamlessly into your social media strategy. Platforms like Facebook, Instagram, and Twitter are ideal for short-form videos, teasers, and promotional content. Leverage each platform's unique features to maximize engagement and reach a broader audience.

Website Integration

Embed videos on your practice's website to enhance user experience. Feature introductory videos on your homepage, educational content on relevant service pages, and patient testimonials on dedicated testimonial pages. Video integration creates a dynamic and engaging online presence.

Analyzing Video Performance

Key Metrics for Evaluation

To grade your video marketing efforts, understand and monitor key metrics. Track metrics such as views, watch time, engagement, and click-through rates. Analyzing these metrics provides insights into viewer behavior and the overall impact of your video content.

Feedback and Comments

Encourage viewer interaction through comments and feedback. Pay attention to audience reactions, questions, and suggestions. Viewer engagement in the form of comments provides valuable insights and an opportunity for your practice to connect directly with your audience.

Video Marketing in Action - A Case Study

Transformative Success Metrics

Let's delve into a hypothetical case study to illustrate the transformative impact of a well-executed video marketing strategy:

- Increased Engagement on Social Media: Strategic use of short-form videos on social media platforms led to a significant increase in engagement, with likes, shares, and comments reaching new heights.

- Elevated Brand Perception: Behind-the-scenes videos showcasing the friendly team and advanced equipment contributed to an enhanced brand perception, making the practice more approachable.

- Positive Patient Feedback: Patient testimonials garnered widespread positive feedback, with viewers expressing trust and confidence in the practice based on the authentic experiences shared by others.

CHAPTER 7

MASTERING DENTAL SEO: A STRATEGIC GUIDE TO AMPLIFY YOUR ONLINE PRESENCE

Understanding the Digital Landscape

In an era where patients turn to the internet to find dental services, understanding the digital landscape is crucial. Dental SEO is the key that unlocks visibility, ensuring your practice is not just present online but easily discoverable by individuals actively seeking dental services.

The Impact of Online Visibility on Patient Acquisition

Online visibility directly correlates with patient acquisition. As your practice climbs the ranks in search engine results, the likelihood of attracting new patients increases exponentially. Dental SEO is not just about ranking; it's about strategically positioning your practice where it matters most—on the first page of search results.

Components of Comprehensive Dental SEO

Optimize Content for Relevance

Content optimization lies at the heart of dental SEO. Craft informative, relevant, and engaging content that caters to the needs of your target audience. From service pages to blog posts, each piece of content should contribute to a cohesive narrative that showcases your expertise and addresses patient queries.

Meta Tags - The Gateway to Search Engines

Meta tags, including title tags and meta descriptions, act as the gateway between your website and search engines. Craft compelling, keyword-rich tags that not only convey the essence of your content but also entice users to click through. Strategic meta tags contribute significantly to higher click-through rates.

Image Optimization for a Seamless Experience

Images play a crucial role in user experience and SEO. Optimize images by compressing them without compromising quality, utilizing descriptive file names, and incorporating alt text. Image optimization not only enhances page load speed but also contributes to improved rankings in image search results.

Quality Backlinks as a Pillar of Authority

Backlinks, or external links from reputable websites to yours, are the backbone of your website's authority. Invest in quality backlinks that are relevant to your dental niche. Each backlink is a vote of confidence in your practice, signaling to search engines that your website is a reliable source of information.

Crafting a Dental SEO Strategy

Keyword Research for Targeted Visibility

Keyword research forms the foundation of a successful dental SEO strategy. Identify relevant keywords that align with your services and are commonly searched by your target audience. Strategically integrate these keywords into your content, meta tags, and headers to enhance search engine visibility.

Local SEO for Geographically Targeted Success

For dental practices, local SEO is paramount. Claim and optimize your Google My Business listing, ensuring accurate business information, consistent NAP (Name, Address, Phone) details, and positive reviews. Local SEO tactics contribute to higher rankings in location-based searches.

Regular Content Updates for Freshness

Search engines favor fresh, relevant content. Regularly update your website with informative blog posts, news articles, and service updates. Fresh content signals to search engines that your website is actively maintained, contributing to higher rankings.

Measuring Dental SEO Success

Key Metrics for Evaluation

To grade your dental SEO efforts, understand and monitor key metrics. Track metrics such as organic traffic, keyword rankings, bounce rates, and conversion rates. Analyzing these metrics provides insights into the performance of your SEO strategy.

Utilizing SEO Tools for In-Depth Analysis

Leverage SEO tools such as Google Analytics, Google Search Console, and third-party platforms for in-depth analysis. These tools provide detailed insights into user behavior, keyword performance, and website health. Use the data to refine and optimize your dental SEO strategy continuously.

Dental SEO in Action - A Case Study

Transformative Success Metrics

Let's delve into a hypothetical case study to illustrate the transformative impact of a well-executed dental SEO strategy:

- Increased Organic Traffic: Strategic optimization resulted in a notable increase in organic traffic, with the practice ranking higher for relevant keywords.

- Enhanced Local Visibility: Local SEO efforts led to improved visibility in location-based searches, attracting a higher volume of nearby patients.

- Improved Conversion Rates: Targeted content and optimized user experience contributed to higher conversion rates, translating website visits into patient appointments.

CHAPTER 8

REVOLUTIONIZING PATIENT EXPERIENCE: A COMPREHENSIVE GUIDE TO IMPLEMENTING ONLINE APPOINTMENT SCHEDULING

Embracing Technological Advancements

In an era where technology shapes every facet of our lives, the healthcare industry is no exception. Embrace the evolution of patient experience by leveraging technological advancements that streamline processes, foster convenience, and elevate the overall satisfaction of those seeking dental services.

The Impact of Convenience on Patient Satisfaction

Convenience is a cornerstone of patient satisfaction. As dental professionals, offering a seamless and convenient appointment scheduling process demonstrates a commitment to meeting the evolving expectations of your patients. Online appointment scheduling serves as a pivotal tool to achieve this level of convenience.

The Advantages of Online Appointment Scheduling

Simplifying the Booking Process

Online appointment scheduling simplifies the booking process for both your team and patients. Eliminate the need for phone calls, back-and-forth conversations, and potential scheduling conflicts. A user-friendly online platform provides a straightforward way for patients to select their preferred time slots, reducing administrative burdens on your end.

24/7 Accessibility

Unlike traditional appointment scheduling that relies on office hours, online scheduling offers 24/7 accessibility. Patients can book appointments at their convenience, whether it's late at night, during weekends, or on holidays. This flexibility aligns with the diverse and dynamic schedules of today's patients.

Minimizing No-Shows and Cancellations

Online scheduling systems often incorporate automated reminders and confirmations, minimizing the occurrence of no-shows and last-minute cancellations. The convenience of receiving timely reminders via email or SMS ensures that patients are more likely to honor their appointments, contributing to a more efficient and predictable schedule for your practice.

Implementing Online Appointment Scheduling

Selecting a User-Friendly Platform

Choose a user-friendly online appointment scheduling platform that aligns with the specific needs and workflows of your dental practice. Consider factors such as ease of use, integration capabilities with your existing systems, and the level of customization available.

Integrating with Practice Management Software

For a seamless operational workflow, integrate your online scheduling platform with your practice management software. This integration ensures that appointments seamlessly sync with your existing scheduling system, minimizing the risk of errors and maintaining a unified patient database.

Customizing Appointment Parameters

Tailor the online scheduling system to reflect the unique parameters of your dental practice. Define appointment types, durations, and any specific requirements for different procedures. Customization ensures that the online platform aligns with the intricacies of your practice's scheduling needs.

Providing Clear Instructions

Ensure that your online scheduling platform provides clear instructions for patients. Offer guidance on selecting the right appointment type, provide any necessary pre-appointment instructions, and offer support channels for those who may need assistance navigating the online scheduling process.

Measuring Success and Optimizing

Key Metrics for Evaluation

To gauge the success of your online appointment scheduling implementation, track key metrics such as appointment booking rates, no-show rates, and patient feedback. Analyzing these metrics provides valuable insights into the efficiency and effectiveness of your online scheduling strategy.

Gathering Patient Feedback

Actively seek feedback from patients regarding their experience with the online scheduling system. Understand their perspectives on usability, clarity of instructions, and overall satisfaction. Patient feedback is invaluable in identifying areas for improvement and optimizing the online scheduling process.

Online Appointment Scheduling in Action - A Case Study

Transformative Success Metrics

Let's delve into a hypothetical case study to illustrate the transformative impact of a well-implemented online appointment scheduling system:

- Increased Appointment Booking Rates: The implementation of online scheduling led to a significant increase in appointment booking rates, with patients embracing the convenience of selecting time slots at their convenience.

- Drastic Reduction in No-Shows: Automated reminders and confirmations resulted in a drastic reduction in no-shows, contributing to a more predictable and efficient schedule.

- Positive Patient Feedback: Patients expressed high satisfaction with the ease of use and accessibility of the online scheduling system, positioning the practice as responsive to their needs.

CHAPTER 9

ELEVATING YOUR DENTAL PRACTICE: THE POWER OF ENGAGING SOCIAL MEDIA CONTESTS.

Understanding the Impact of Social Media

In an age dominated by digital communication, social media stands as a powerful tool to connect with your audience. Understanding the impact of social media on patient engagement and brand visibility is crucial for leveraging its full potential.

The Role of Engagement in Building a Digital Community

Engagement is the heartbeat of a thriving digital community. As dental professionals, your social media presence goes beyond mere promotion; it's about building a community where patients feel connected, informed, and actively involved in the narrative of your practice.

The Advantages of Social Media Contests

Boosting Audience Engagement

Social media contests serve as catalysts for audience engagement. By tapping into the human desire for competition and reward, contests encourage your audience to actively participate through likes, shares, comments, and other interactive actions.

Broadening Social Media Reach

Contests have a viral potential. When participants engage with your content, it expands the reach of your posts to their networks. As friends of participants see and interact with contest-related content, your practice gains exposure to a broader audience, amplifying the impact of your social media presence.

Fostering a Sense of Community

Contests foster a sense of community among your online audience. Whether it's a photo contest, a quiz, or a creative challenge, participants become part of a collective experience. This shared participation strengthens the bond between your practice and your digital community.

Planning Engaging Social Media Contests

Identifying Contest Objectives

Before launching a social media contest, define your objectives. Whether it's increasing brand awareness, promoting a new service, or simply fostering community engagement, having clear goals will guide the structure and execution of your contest.

Choosing the Right Contest Format

Social media contests come in various formats, each catering to different objectives. Consider options such as photo contests, caption contests, trivia quizzes, or user-generated content challenges. Tailor the format to align with your goals and resonate with your audience.

Defining Clear Rules and Guidelines

Transparency is key in contest planning. Clearly outline the rules, guidelines, and eligibility criteria for participation. This not only ensures a fair and structured contest but also builds trust among your audience.

Implementing and Promoting Social Media Contests

Leveraging Visual Appeal

Humans are visual beings, and your contest should reflect this. Use eye-catching visuals, graphics, and videos to promote your contest. Visual appeal not only attracts attention but also conveys the excitement and energy of the contest.

Utilizing Relevant Hashtags

Hashtags are powerful tools to amplify the reach of your contest. Create a unique and relevant hashtag for your contest, encouraging participants to use it in their submissions. This not only organizes entries but also facilitates easy tracking and promotion.

Cross-Promoting Across Platforms

Extend the reach of your contest by cross-promoting across multiple social media platforms. Share teasers, updates, and winner announcements across platforms to ensure your entire digital audience is engaged.

Measuring the Success of Social Media Contests

Key Metrics for Evaluation

To gauge the success of your social media contests, track key metrics such as engagement rates, follower growth, and the overall reach of your contest-related content. Analyzing these metrics provides valuable insights into the effectiveness of your contest strategy.

Gathering Participant Feedback

Actively seek feedback from contest participants. Understand their perspectives on the contest format, rules, and overall experience. Participant feedback is invaluable in identifying areas for improvement and tailoring future contests to better resonate with your audience.

Social Media Contests in Action - A Case Study

Transformative Success Metrics

Let's delve into a hypothetical case study to illustrate the transformative impact of well-executed social media contests:

- Surge in Engagement: A carefully planned contest led to a significant surge in engagement, with participants actively liking, sharing, and commenting on contest-related content.

- Substantial Follower Growth: The viral nature of the contest content contributed to substantial follower growth, expanding the practice's digital community.

- Positive Community Sentiment: Participant feedback reflected positive sentiments, with many expressing enthusiasm for future contests and a heightened sense of connection with the dental practice.

CHAPTER 10

MASTERING DENTAL MARKETING: THE ART OF EDUCATIONAL WEBINARS AND WORKSHOPS

Unveiling the Power of Educational Marketing

Understanding the Educational Paradigm

In an era where information is abundant, educational marketing stands as a beacon of value. Understanding the educational paradigm is crucial for dental professionals looking to position themselves as trusted sources of knowledge in the digital landscape.

The Impact of Expertise on Patient Trust

Expertise breeds trust. As dental professionals, showcasing your knowledge not only enhances your credibility within the industry but also fosters trust among current and potential patients. Educational webinars and workshops serve as dynamic platforms to convey your expertise.

The Advantages of Educational Webinars and Workshops

Establishing Authority in the Industry

Hosting webinars and workshops positions you as an authority in the dental industry. Covering a range of topics, from oral health tips to cutting-edge advancements, establishes your practice as a go-to resource for valuable information.

Building a Community of Engaged Patients

Educational content fosters a sense of community among your audience. Patients who engage with your webinars and workshops become part of a knowledge-sharing community, enhancing their connection to your practice beyond routine dental appointments.

Leveraging Online Accessibility

Webinars and online workshops offer unparalleled accessibility. With the power of digital platforms, you can reach a global audience, expanding the impact of your educational initiatives beyond the confines of your local community.

Planning and Executing Educational Webinars

Identifying Target Topics

Before diving into webinar planning, identify topics that align with your expertise and cater to the interests of your audience. Whether it's demystifying dental procedures or exploring emerging trends, tailor your content to resonate with your target demographic.

Choosing the Right Format

Webinars come in various formats, such as lectures, panel discussions, and interactive Q&A sessions. Choose a format that suits your content and engages your audience effectively. Variety keeps your educational initiatives dynamic and captivating.

Promoting Your Webinars

Effective promotion is key to a successful webinar. Utilize your existing digital platforms, including social media, newsletters, and your practice website, to promote upcoming webinars. Clearly communicate the value participants will gain from attending.

Hosting Engaging Online Workshops

Crafting Workshop Curriculums

Workshops require structured curriculums that balance information dissemination with interactive elements.

Design a curriculum that encourages participation, hands-on learning, and active engagement from your audience.

Utilizing Interactive Tools

Leverage interactive tools such as polls, quizzes, and live Q&A sessions during online workshops. These tools not only keep participants engaged but also provide valuable insights into their understanding of the material.

Ensuring Technical Accessibility

Technical hiccups can hinder the success of online workshops. Ensure that your chosen platform is user-friendly, compatible with various devices, and offers technical support for both hosts and participants.

Measuring the Impact of Educational Initiatives

Tracking Participant Engagement

Measure the success of your educational webinars and workshops by tracking participant engagement. Analyze metrics such as attendance rates, interaction levels, and post-event surveys to gauge the effectiveness of your initiatives.

Assessing Social Media Reach

Webinars and workshops often generate social media buzz. Assess the reach and impact of your educational content by tracking social media metrics, including likes, shares, and comments. Social media analytics provide valuable insights into the resonance of your educational initiatives.

Educational Initiatives in Action - A Case Study

Transformative Success Metrics

Let's delve into a hypothetical case study to illustrate the transformative impact of well-executed educational initiatives:

- Increased Online Presence: Educational webinars and workshops led to a substantial increase in the practice's online presence, positioning them as thought leaders in the dental industry.

- Enhanced Patient Loyalty: Engaged participants expressed a heightened sense of loyalty to the practice, viewing it not only as a provider of dental services but also as a valuable source of dental knowledge.

- Positive Community Feedback: Participants and online viewers provided positive feedback, highlighting the value they gained from the educational content and expressing anticipation for future initiatives.

CHAPTER 11

NAVIGATING THE REALM OF DENTAL MARKETING: A COMPREHENSIVE GUIDE TO INFLUENCER MARKETING

Decoding the Essence of Influencer Marketing

Unveiling the Influence Phenomenon

In an era dominated by digital communication, influencers have emerged as powerful voices shaping consumer opinions. Understanding the essence of influencer marketing is pivotal for dental professionals looking to harness the authentic appeal of these influential figures.

The Impact of Authentic Endorsements

Authenticity is the cornerstone of effective influencer marketing. When influencers authentically endorse your dental practice, their followers perceive the recommendation as genuine and trustworthy. This impact extends beyond traditional marketing strategies, forging a connection that resonates with potential patients.

The Advantages of Influencer Marketing

Elevating Credibility in the Dental Space

Collaborating with influencers in the dental and healthcare space elevates your practice's credibility. Their endorsement serves as a powerful validation, positioning your practice as a trusted authority within the industry.

Tapping into Diverse Audiences

Influencers boast diverse follower bases, each with unique interests and demographics. Collaborating with influencers allows your practice to tap into these varied audiences, expanding your reach to potential patients who align with your values and services.

Amplifying Online Reach

Influencers wield the ability to amplify your online reach significantly. Leveraging their existing followers, influencer collaborations extend your practice's visibility across social media platforms, fostering brand awareness and engagement.

Identifying Ideal Influencer Collaborations

Aligning with Dental and Healthcare Influencers

Choose influencers whose content aligns with the dental and healthcare niche. Collaborating with influencers who share relevant insights and industry-related content ensures that their endorsement seamlessly integrates with your practice's messaging.

Assessing Authenticity and Engagement

Authenticity and engagement are paramount in influencer collaborations. Evaluate influencers based on the authenticity of their endorsements, genuine engagement with their audience, and the resonance of their content with your practice's values.

Exploring Micro-Influencer Partnerships

Consider exploring partnerships with micro-influencers, who may have smaller but highly engaged follower bases. Micro-influencers often offer a more personalized touch and can foster meaningful connections with their audience.

Crafting Effective Influencer Campaigns

Defining Clear Objectives

Before initiating influencer collaborations, define clear objectives for your campaigns. Whether it's increasing brand awareness, promoting specific services, or attracting new patients, having well-defined goals guides the structure and execution of your influencer campaigns.

Tailoring Campaign Messages

Collaborate closely with influencers to tailor campaign messages that align with your practice's values and objectives. Ensure that the content resonates authentically with their audience while effectively conveying your practice's unique selling points.

Utilizing Diverse Content Formats

Influencer campaigns thrive on diverse content formats. Encourage influencers to create engaging content such as testimonials, behind-the-scenes glimpses, and interactive Q&A sessions. Varied content formats enhance the overall impact of your campaigns.

Measuring the Success of Influencer Campaigns

Tracking Key Performance Indicators (KPIs)

To gauge the success of influencer campaigns, track key performance indicators (KPIs) such as reach, engagement, and conversion rates. Analyzing these metrics provides valuable insights into the effectiveness of your influencer collaborations.

Gathering Patient Feedback

Actively seek feedback from patients who discovered your practice through influencer campaigns. Understand their perspectives on the influencer collaboration, and assess whether it positively influenced their decision to engage with your practice.

Influencer Campaigns in Action - A Case Study

Transformative Success Metrics

Let's delve into a hypothetical case study to illustrate the transformative impact of well-executed influencer campaigns:

- Exponential Online Reach: A strategically planned influencer campaign led to a significant increase in the practice's online reach, reaching thousands of potential patients who resonated with the influencer's authentic endorsement.

- Enhanced Brand Recognition: The collaboration elevated the practice's brand recognition, with the influencer's followers associating the practice with credibility and trustworthiness in the dental space.

- Positive Community Engagement: The influencer campaign fostered positive engagement within the dental community, leading to increased interaction, inquiries, and appointments from individuals who discovered the practice through the collaboration.

CHAPTER 12

NAVIGATING THE MOBILE REVOLUTION: A COMPREHENSIVE GUIDE TO OPTIMIZING YOUR DENTAL MARKETING FOR MOBILE PLATFORMS

Embracing the Mobile Revolution

The Mobile Device Phenomenon

In an era where smartphones are ubiquitous, understanding the significance of the mobile revolution is essential. Mobile devices have become an integral part of our daily lives, influencing how we communicate, access information, and make decisions.

The Impact on Patient Behavior

Recognizing the impact of mobile devices on patient behavior is key to crafting an effective mobile marketing strategy. Patients use their smartphones to research healthcare providers, book appointments, and engage with healthcare-related content. Optimizing for mobile ensures your practice remains accessible and relevant in the eyes of your digitally-savvy audience.

The Advantages of Mobile Optimization

Enhanced Accessibility

Optimizing your dental marketing for mobile platforms ensures enhanced accessibility for your audience. Patients can seamlessly access your website, read content, and engage with your practice on-the-go, fostering a user-friendly experience.

Improved User Experience

Mobile optimization goes beyond responsive design; it encompasses creating an optimal user experience. Streamlined navigation, fast loading times, and intuitive interfaces on mobile devices contribute to a positive user experience, increasing patient satisfaction.

Increased Patient Engagement

Engaging patients through mobile-friendly content, SMS marketing, and interactive features enhances overall patient engagement. By meeting patients where they are – on their mobile devices – you foster a connection that aligns with their preferences and habits.

Crafting a Mobile-Friendly Strategy

Responsive Web Design

Implementing responsive web design is the foundation of a mobile-friendly strategy. Ensure your practice website adapts seamlessly to various screen sizes, providing an optimal viewing experience across devices. This not only caters to patient convenience but also positively impacts your website's search engine rankings.

SMS Marketing Tactics

Leveraging SMS marketing is a direct way to connect with patients on their mobile devices. Craft concise, engaging messages that convey important information, appointment reminders, and promotions. SMS marketing adds a personal touch and ensures your messages are promptly delivered and read.

Mobile-Friendly Content Creation

Tailoring your content for mobile consumption is crucial. Patients often engage with bite-sized content on their smartphones. Ensure your website content, blog posts, and educational materials are concise, visually appealing, and easy to navigate on smaller screens.

Technical Aspects of Mobile Optimization

Page Speed Optimization

Mobile users prioritize speed. Optimize your website's loading times to cater to impatient mobile users. Compress images, leverage browser caching, and minimize server response times to create a seamless and fast mobile experience.

Mobile SEO Best Practices

Implementing mobile SEO best practices ensures your practice remains visible in mobile search results. This includes optimizing meta tags, utilizing mobile-friendly keywords, and creating a mobile XML sitemap. A strong mobile SEO foundation contributes to your practice's overall online visibility.

Mobile-Friendly Forms

If your practice uses online forms for appointment scheduling or patient inquiries, ensure these forms are mobile-friendly. Simplify form fields, use auto-fill options, and optimize the submission process to create a frictionless experience for mobile users.

Measuring Mobile Success

Tracking Mobile Analytics

Monitoring mobile analytics provides insights into the success of your mobile optimization efforts. Track metrics such as mobile traffic, bounce rates, and conversion rates specifically for mobile users. This data helps in refining your strategy based on user behavior.

Gathering Patient Feedback

Actively seek feedback from patients regarding their mobile experience with your practice. Surveys or feedback forms can provide valuable insights into areas that may require further optimization. Patient feedback ensures your mobile strategy aligns with their expectations and preferences.

Mobile Optimization in Action - A Case Study

Transformative Success Metrics

Let's delve into a hypothetical case study to illustrate the transformative impact of a well-executed mobile optimization strategy:

- Increased Mobile Traffic: A comprehensive mobile optimization strategy led to a significant increase in mobile traffic to the practice website, showcasing the effectiveness of responsive design and mobile-friendly content.

- Improved Patient Engagement: Mobile-specific campaigns, including SMS marketing and interactive content, contributed to heightened patient engagement. Patients actively participated in promotions and responded positively to mobile-friendly communication.

- Enhanced Appointment Bookings: The simplified mobile appointment booking process resulted in an uptick in mobile users scheduling appointments through the practice website. A streamlined user journey contributed to increased conversion rates

CHAPTER 13

CRAFTING PERSONALIZED PATIENT JOURNEYS: A COMPREHENSIVE GUIDE TO OPTIMIZING DENTAL MARKETING THROUGH TARGETED LANDING PAGES

Unraveling the Power of Targeted Landing Pages

The Significance of Personalization

Understanding the significance of personalization in dental marketing is paramount. Targeted landing pages serve as a personalized entry point for patients, offering a tailored experience that resonates with their specific needs and interests.

From General to Targeted: The Evolution of Patient Journeys

Traditionally, dental marketing may have focused on general messaging for a broad audience. However, the evolution towards targeted landing pages signifies a shift towards creating specific patient journeys tailored to individual preferences and concerns.

Advantages of Targeted Landing Pages

Increased Patient Engagement

Targeted landing pages foster increased patient engagement by providing content and offers specifically relevant to the patient's interests. This personal touch creates a more meaningful interaction, capturing attention and encouraging further exploration.

Higher Conversion Rates

A tailored approach significantly increases the likelihood of patient conversion. By addressing specific needs or promoting services relevant to a particular audience segment, targeted landing pages guide patients towards taking desired actions, whether it's scheduling an appointment, signing up for a newsletter, or exploring specific treatments.

Enhanced User Experience

Patient experience is elevated through targeted landing pages, offering a seamless and relevant journey. Visitors feel more understood and valued when the content they encounter aligns with their interests, leading to a positive perception of your practice.

Crafting Effective Targeted Landing Pages

Identifying Audience Segments

The first step in creating targeted landing pages is identifying distinct audience segments. Analyze your patient base, considering demographics, preferences, and common concerns. This segmentation forms the foundation for personalized content creation.

Aligning Content with Patient Needs

Craft content that directly addresses the needs and interests of each identified audience segment. Whether it's highlighting specific services, promotions, or addressing common dental concerns, align the content to resonate with the intended audience.

Designing User-Friendly Pages

Optimize the design of your landing pages for a user-friendly experience. Ensure easy navigation, compelling visuals, and clear calls-to-action. A well-designed landing page enhances the overall user experience, guiding patients seamlessly through the desired journey.

Technical Aspects of Targeted Landing Pages

Utilizing Dynamic Content

Explore the use of dynamic content on your landing pages. Dynamic elements, such as personalized greetings, tailored offers, or location-specific information, add a layer of customization that captivates the audience's attention and encourages engagement.

Implementing A/B Testing

Refine the effectiveness of your targeted landing pages through A/B testing. Experiment with different headlines, visuals, or calls-to-action to identify the elements that resonate most with your audience. Continuous testing ensures ongoing optimization for maximum impact.

Integrating with Analytics Tools

Integrate your targeted landing pages with analytics tools to track user behavior and engagement. Analyzing metrics such as bounce rates, time spent on page, and conversion rates provides valuable insights into the performance of your personalized patient journeys.

Measuring Success

Tracking Conversion Metrics

Measure the success of your targeted landing pages by tracking conversion metrics. Monitor the number of appointments scheduled, forms submitted, or other desired actions taken by patients. Analyzing these metrics provides a clear understanding of the impact of your personalized patient journeys.

Gathering Patient Feedback

Actively seek feedback from patients who engaged with targeted landing pages. Surveys or feedback forms can reveal insights into the patient experience, helping you fine-tune your approach and address specific preferences.

Targeted Landing Pages in Action - A Case Study

Transformative Success Metrics

Let's explore a hypothetical case study to illustrate the transformative impact of well-crafted targeted landing pages:

- Increased Appointment Requests: A targeted landing page promoting a specific dental service led to a significant increase in appointment requests from patients interested in that particular treatment.

- Tailored Offers for New Patients: An exclusive promotion for new patients, highlighted on a dedicated landing page, resulted in a surge of inquiries and appointment bookings from individuals seeking to take advantage of the personalized offer.

- Positive Patient Feedback: Patients who engaged with targeted landing pages expressed satisfaction with the personalized content and offers, emphasizing the practice's commitment to understanding their unique needs.

CHAPTER 14

CRAFTING A COMPREHENSIVE PATIENT EDUCATION HUB: ELEVATING YOUR PRACTICE AS AN AUTHORITY IN ORAL HEALTH

Understanding the Significance of Patient Education

The Power of Informed Patients

Recognizing the power of informed patients is the cornerstone of successful dental marketing. Educated patients are more engaged, proactive, and likely to make informed decisions regarding their oral health.

The Impact of Patient Education on Practice Reputation

Understanding how patient education directly impacts your practice's reputation is vital. By providing valuable information, you position your practice as a reliable source, fostering trust and credibility among your patient base.

Advantages of an Online Patient Education Hub

Empowering Patients with Knowledge

An online patient education hub empowers patients by providing them with accessible, reliable information. This empowerment leads to better decision-making and a proactive approach to oral health.

Building Trust and Credibility

Being a go-to resource for oral health information builds trust and credibility. Patients are more likely to choose a practice they perceive as knowledgeable and invested in their well-being.

Strengthening the Patient-Provider Relationship

Engaging patients through educational content strengthens the relationship between the dental practice and its clientele. Patients appreciate practices that go beyond clinical services, fostering a connection that extends beyond appointments.

Crafting an Effective Patient Education Hub

Identifying Key Educational Topics

Begin by identifying key topics relevant to your patient demographic. Consider common dental concerns, preventive care tips, and emerging trends in oral health. Tailor your content to address the specific needs and interests of your audience.

Diversifying Content Formats

Diversify your content to cater to different learning preferences. Incorporate blog posts, articles, infographics, videos, and downloadable guides. Offering a variety of formats ensures your patient education hub appeals to a broad audience.

Creating User-Friendly Content

Ensure your educational content is user-friendly. Optimize readability, use clear visuals, and present information in a digestible format. A user-friendly approach enhances the overall experience for your audience.

Technical Aspects of Building an Education Hub

Responsive Design for Accessibility

Implement responsive design to make your patient education hub accessible across various devices. Whether patients access your content on a desktop, tablet, or smartphone, responsive design ensures a consistent and user-friendly experience.

Multimedia Optimization

When incorporating multimedia elements like videos and infographics, ensure they are optimized for various devices. Optimize file sizes, use formats compatible with different platforms, and test functionality to guarantee a seamless experience.

Analytics Integration for Continuous Improvement

Integrate analytics tools to track user engagement with your educational content. Monitor metrics such as page views, time spent on pages, and click-through rates to understand which topics resonate most with your audience. Analytics provide valuable insights for refining your content strategy.

Measuring Success and Impact

Analyzing User Feedback

Actively seek feedback from patients regarding your educational content. Surveys, comments, and social media interactions can reveal insights into the impact of your educational efforts. Use this feedback to refine your content and address specific patient interests.

Tracking Knowledge Retention

Assess the knowledge retention of your patients by incorporating quizzes or surveys into your educational content. Monitor how well patients retain and apply the information provided, allowing you to tailor future content to address areas where additional clarification may be needed.

Patient Education Hub in Action - A Case Study

Transformative Success Metrics

Let's explore a hypothetical case study to illustrate the transformative impact of a well-established patient education hub:

- Increased Patient Engagement: The introduction of a patient education hub led to a notable increase in website engagement, with patients spending more time exploring informative content.

- Positive Patient Feedback: Patients expressed appreciation for the valuable insights provided through the education hub. The practice received positive feedback, emphasizing the impact of becoming a trusted source of oral health knowledge.

- Enhanced Preventive Care: Patients who engaged with educational content demonstrated a heightened awareness of preventive care measures, leading to improved oral health practices and a decrease in dental issues.

CHAPTER 15

ELEVATING YOUR DENTAL MARKETING: A COMPREHENSIVE GUIDE TO MASTERING GOOGLE ADS REMARKETING

Unveiling the Potential of Google Ads Remarketing

Understanding the Remarketing Landscape

To effectively grade your own marketing strategy, it's crucial to understand the fundamental dynamics of Google Ads Remarketing. This strategy revolves around reconnecting with users who have previously visited your website. The subtle reminder presented through remarketing campaigns aims to keep your dental practice in the forefront of their minds, potentially influencing them to revisit and schedule appointments.

The Psychology Behind Remarketing

Delve into the psychology behind remarketing. Research indicates that subtle reminders play a pivotal role in decision-making. Remarketing operates as a gentle nudge, fostering familiarity and trust, thereby prompting users to take the desired action—scheduling crucial dental appointments.

Advantages of Google Ads Remarketing

Increased Brand Recall

One of the primary advantages of Google Ads remarketing is the substantial increase in brand recall. By consistently appearing in front of users who have expressed interest in your practice, you reinforce your brand, making it more likely that they'll choose your services over competitors.

Targeted Messaging

Google Ads remarketing empowers you to tailor your messaging based on users' past interactions with your website. Whether they explored specific services or browsed particular pages, you can craft targeted ads that speak directly to their interests and needs, increasing the relevance of your communication.

Enhanced Conversion Rates

Studies suggest that remarketing can significantly boost conversion rates. Users who are already familiar with your practice are more likely to convert into patients. Remarketing ensures your practice remains on their radar, increasing the chances of converting interest into action.

Crafting an Effective Google Ads Remarketing Strategy

Setting Clear Objectives

To gauge the effectiveness of your remarketing strategy, set clear objectives. Whether your primary goal is to increase appointment bookings, promote specific services, or encourage consultations, having well-defined objectives guides the entire strategy.

Segmenting Your Audience

Effective remarketing involves segmenting your audience based on their past interactions with your website. Create segments for users who visited specific service pages, those who abandoned appointment scheduling, and others. This segmentation allows for personalized and relevant remarketing messages.

Tailoring Ad Creatives

Craft compelling ad creatives that align with your audience segments. Tailor your messaging to address their specific needs and concerns. Personalization is key to capturing their attention and prompting them to take the next step in their patient journey.

Technical Aspects of Google Ads Remarketing

Installing the Google Remarketing Tag

Ensure the proper installation of the Google Remarketing Tag on your website. This tag allows Google to track user interactions and deliver targeted ads. Verify that the tag is correctly implemented across all relevant pages to ensure accurate tracking.

Utilizing Dynamic Remarketing

Explore the use of dynamic remarketing to showcase specific services or products that users viewed on your website. Dynamic ads automatically populate with relevant content, enhancing the personalization of your remarketing efforts.

Frequency Capping

Implementing frequency capping is crucial to controlling how often users see your remarketing ads. While consistent visibility is crucial, striking a balance prevents overexposure, ensuring your ads remain effective without becoming intrusive.

Measuring Success

Monitoring Key Metrics

Regularly monitor key metrics to gauge the success of your Google Ads remarketing campaigns. Track metrics such as click-through rates, conversion rates, and return on ad spend (ROAS) to assess performance and identify areas for improvement.

Analyzing Audience Engagement

Dive into audience engagement metrics to understand how users are interacting with your remarketing ads. Analyze the performance of different audience segments, ad creatives, and messaging variations to refine your approach.

Google Ads Remarketing in Action - A Case Study

Transformative Success Metrics

Let's explore a hypothetical case study to illustrate the transformative impact of a well-executed Google Ads remarketing strategy:

- Significant Increase in Appointment Bookings: A dental practice implemented remarketing campaigns targeting users who had shown interest in specific treatments. This resulted in a substantial increase in appointment bookings from the remarketed audience.

- Enhanced ROI on Ad Spend: By optimizing ad creatives and audience segments, the practice achieved a higher return on ad spend. Remarketing proved to be a cost-effective strategy, delivering measurable results.

- Positive Patient Feedback: Users who engaged with the remarketing campaigns expressed positive sentiments about the personalized content. The practice received favorable feedback, emphasizing the impact of staying connected through targeted ads.

CHAPTER 16TH

MASTERING VOICE SEARCH OPTIMIZATION: NAVIGATING THE FUTURE OF DENTAL MARKETING

Decoding the Rise of Voice Search

Unveiling the Surge in Voice-Activated Devices

To effectively grade your marketing strategy, it's essential to understand the surge in voice-activated devices. Smart speakers, virtual assistants, and mobile devices equipped with voice recognition technology have become ubiquitous. Users now rely on these devices to seek information, make inquiries, and even schedule appointments.

The Shift in Search Behavior

A seismic shift is underway in search behavior. Traditional text-based queries are giving way to conversational, voice-driven searches. Users, seeking convenience, now articulate queries as they would in a conversation. To adapt, your dental practice must optimize for this shift by embracing voice search optimization strategies.

The Significance of Voice Search Optimization

Anticipating User Needs

One of the primary advantages of voice search optimization is its ability to anticipate user needs. By understanding the context of voice queries, your practice can provide more accurate and relevant information. This anticipation is crucial in meeting the expectations of patients seeking prompt and precise answers.

Enhancing Accessibility

Optimizing for voice search enhances the accessibility of your dental practice. Users can engage with your online content hands-free, making it more convenient for those inquiring about your services while multitasking or in situations where manual interaction is limited.

Capturing Local Voice Searches

Voice searches often have a local intent. Users frequently ask about nearby dental services or inquire about specific treatments available in their area. Voice search optimization ensures your practice is visible and well-positioned to capture these local inquiries.

Crafting a Voice Search-Optimized Strategy

Conversational Keyword Research

Embark on a journey of conversational keyword research. Unlike traditional search queries, voice searches mimic natural language. Identify and integrate conversational keywords into your content, anticipating the questions your patients might pose when using voice-activated devices.

Providing Concise and Informative Answers

Voice search queries often seek concise and informative answers. Craft content that directly addresses common inquiries, offering clear and relevant information. By aligning your content with the expectations of voice search users, your practice becomes a go-to source for valuable insights.

Structuring Content for Featured Snippets

Voice-activated devices often pull information from featured snippets when responding to queries. Structure your online content to qualify for featured snippets by providing succinct answers and organizing information in a format that aligns with the preferences of voice search algorithms.

Technical Aspects of Voice Search Optimization

Schema Markup Implementation

Integrate schema markup to provide search engines with structured information about your practice. This technical enhancement enables voice search algorithms to extract and present relevant details, ensuring your practice is accurately represented in voice search results.

Mobile Optimization

Given the prevalence of voice search on mobile devices, prioritize mobile optimization. Ensure that your website is responsive, loads quickly, and provides a seamless experience for users engaging with voice search features on their smartphones.

Local SEO for Voice Searches

Elevate your local SEO game for voice searches. Claim and optimize your Google My Business listing, use location-specific keywords, and encourage satisfied patients to leave positive reviews. Local SEO strategies tailored for voice search ensure your practice is prominently featured in relevant local queries.

Measuring Success

Analyzing Voice Search Traffic

To grade the effectiveness of your voice search optimization, analyze the traffic generated from voice searches. Monitor key metrics such as the volume of voice search queries, user engagement, and the conversion rates of patients who discovered your practice through voice-activated devices.

Evaluating Position Zero Rankings

Voice searches often prioritize information from position zero, also known as featured snippets. Evaluate your practice's position zero rankings for relevant queries. Climbing to the top of position zero enhances your visibility in voice search results.

Voice Search Optimization in Action - A Case Study

Transformative Success Metrics

Embark on a hypothetical case study to understand the transformative impact of a well-executed voice search optimization strategy:

- Increased Visibility in Local Voice Searches: A dental practice implemented local SEO strategies tailored for voice searches, resulting in increased visibility in queries related to dental services in their specific location.

- Enhanced Patient Engagement: By providing concise and informative answers to common dental queries, the practice experienced enhanced patient engagement. Users appreciated the convenience of obtaining relevant information through voice searches.

- Positioned as a Voice Search Authority: Through structured content and schema markup, the practice positioned itself as an authority in voice search results, attracting patients seeking reliable information through voice-activated devices.

CHAPTER 17

BUILDING COMMUNITY CONNECTIONS: A GUIDE TO STRENGTHENING YOUR DENTAL PRACTICE THROUGH LOCAL COLLABORATIONS

Embracing the Local Business Network

Understanding the Importance of Local Collaborations

To effectively grade your marketing strategy, it's crucial to understand the profound impact of local collaborations. Building connections with nearby businesses transcends mere marketing—it's about weaving a fabric of community support that benefits everyone involved. By collaborating, you tap into shared resources, audiences, and goodwill.

The Ripple Effect of Community Ties

Local collaborations create a ripple effect that extends beyond the immediate partnership. When your dental practice actively engages with other businesses, it contributes to a thriving local ecosystem. This, in turn, can lead to increased patient loyalty, positive word-of-mouth, and a solid reputation as a community-centric practice.

The Benefits of Collaborating with Local Businesses

Expanding Your Reach

One of the primary advantages of collaborating with local businesses is the expansion of your reach. By tapping into their existing customer base and vice versa, both parties benefit from exposure to new audiences. Cross-promotions and joint initiatives amplify your visibility within the community.

Strengthening Community Ties

Collaborative efforts strengthen the fabric of the community. Whether it's sponsoring a local event, participating in joint marketing campaigns, or co-hosting initiatives, your dental practice becomes an integral part of the community narrative. This strengthens ties and fosters a positive perception among local residents.

Shared Resources and Cost-Efficiency

Pooling resources with local businesses results in cost-efficient initiatives. Shared marketing campaigns, joint events, or co-branded materials reduce individual financial burdens while maximizing impact. This collaborative approach allows your practice to achieve more with less, creating a win-win scenario for all involved.

Strategies for Successful Local Collaborations

Identifying Compatible Partnerships

To effectively grade your collaborative efforts, identify partnerships that align with your practice's values and goals. Seek out businesses that share a similar target audience but are not direct competitors. For example, partnering with a fitness studio, nutritionist, or wellness center can be synergistic.

Crafting Mutually Beneficial Initiatives

Successful collaborations are rooted in mutual benefit. Craft initiatives that not only promote your dental practice but also add value to your partner's business. This could range from joint promotions and discounts to co-hosted community events that enhance the overall experience for local residents.

Leveraging Digital Platforms for Cross-Promotion

In the digital age, cross-promotion extends beyond physical collaborations. Utilize social media, email newsletters, and collaborative blog posts to amplify your joint efforts. By leveraging digital platforms, you not only reach a broader audience but also enhance the online presence of both businesses.

Measuring the Impact of Local Collaborations

Analyzing Foot Traffic and Patient Acquisition

To grade the success of your local collaborations, analyze foot traffic and patient acquisition during and after joint initiatives. Track the number of new patients attributed to collaborative efforts and assess the impact on your practice's overall growth.

Monitoring Social Media Engagement

Social media provides a tangible metric for gauging collaborative success. Monitor engagement metrics such as likes, shares, and comments on collaborative posts. Positive interactions indicate community interest and involvement, reflecting the success of your joint endeavors.

Realizing the Potential - A Case Study

Transformative Impact on Patient Engagement

Embark on a hypothetical case study to understand the transformative impact of successful local collaborations:

- Community Health Fair: A dental practice collaborates with a local gym, a health food store, and a wellness clinic to organize a community health fair. The event attracts a diverse audience interested in health and well-being. The dental practice offers free oral health check-ups, distributes informative materials, and provides exclusive discounts for attendees.

- Increased Patient Engagement: The collaborative health fair not only attracts new patients but also enhances engagement with existing ones. Attendees appreciate the holistic approach to health, strengthening the bond between the dental practice and the community.

- Positive Brand Perception: The event generates positive publicity, portraying the dental practice as a community-oriented healthcare provider. This positive brand perception contributes to increased trust and loyalty among patients.

CHAPTER 18

MASTERING SOCIAL MEDIA RETARGETING: A COMPREHENSIVE GUIDE FOR DENTAL PRACTICES

Unveiling the Power of Social Media Retargeting

Understanding the Essence of Retargeting

Before we dive into the grading process, let's demystify the concept of retargeting. Social media retargeting involves displaying ads to individuals who have previously interacted with your website or digital content. It's a strategic way to stay in your patient's feed, subtly nudging them towards further engagement.

The Gentle Reminder Approach

Unlike traditional advertising, retargeting ads adopt a gentle reminder approach. These ads reappear on social media platforms, reminding users of your dental practice after they've visited your website or engaged with your online content. The goal is to stay top-of-mind, fostering familiarity and nudging them towards scheduling appointments or engaging with your services.

Crafting Effective Retargeting Ads

Tailoring Your Message

To grade your current retargeting strategy, evaluate the tailoring of your message. Are your ads personalized to the user's previous interactions? Tailoring the message creates a sense of continuity, making the user feel recognized and valued.

Utilizing Compelling Visuals

Visual appeal plays a pivotal role in the effectiveness of retargeting ads. Assess the visual elements of your ads—do they captivate attention? Compelling visuals, coupled with a clear call-to-action, enhance the overall impact and encourage users to take the desired next step.

Diversifying Ad Formats

Retargeting ads come in various formats, including image ads, carousel ads, and video ads. Grading your strategy involves assessing the diversity of your ad formats.

Experimenting with different formats can cater to a broader audience and keep your approach dynamic.

Platforms for Social Media Retargeting

Facebook Retargeting

Facebook is a powerhouse for retargeting ads due to its extensive user base and robust advertising features. Grade your Facebook retargeting strategy by assessing the frequency, relevance, and engagement metrics of your ads within the platform.

Instagram Retargeting

Given its visual-centric nature, Instagram offers a unique canvas for retargeting ads. Evaluate your Instagram retargeting efforts by considering the alignment of your ads with the platform's aesthetics and the resonance with your target audience.

Grading Your Retargeting Performance

Analyzing Click-Through Rates (CTR)

One key metric for grading your retargeting performance is the click-through rate (CTR). Analyze how many users, after being exposed to retargeting ads, click through to your website or landing page. A higher CTR signifies an effective strategy.

Assessing Conversion Rates

Ultimately, the success of retargeting lies in conversions. Evaluate how many users, after interacting with retargeting ads, convert into patients or schedule appointments. A robust retargeting strategy should positively impact conversion rates.

Realizing the Potential - A Case Study

Transformative Impact on Appointment Scheduling

Let's explore a hypothetical case study to illustrate the transformative impact of a successful social media retargeting strategy:

- User Engagement: A potential patient visits your website, explores services, but doesn't schedule an appointment.

- Retargeting Ads: Subsequently, retargeting ads featuring personalized messages and enticing visuals appear on their Facebook and Instagram feeds.

- Increased Engagement: The user, reminded of your practice, clicks on the retargeting ad, leading them back to your website.

- Scheduled Appointment: Motivated by the gentle reminders and personalized approach, the user decides to schedule an appointment, becoming a new patient.

CHAPTER 19

ELEVATING YOUR DENTAL MARKETING STRATEGY: A GUIDE TO DATA-DRIVEN EXCELLENCE

The Foundation of Success - Understanding Data-Driven Decision Making

Unveiling the Importance of Data Analysis

Before delving into the grading process, let's establish a fundamental understanding of why data-driven decision-making is the cornerstone of successful dental marketing. Data analysis provides valuable insights into the performance of your online presence, allowing you to identify trends, gauge user behavior, and adapt strategies accordingly.

The Holistic Approach to Marketing Metrics

Evaluate the various metrics that contribute to the holistic assessment of your marketing efforts. From website analytics to social media insights and advertising platform data, each metric serves as a puzzle piece in the larger picture of your practice's online performance.

Crafting a Grading Framework

Identifying Key Performance Indicators (KPIs)

To effectively grade your marketing strategies, pinpoint the key performance indicators (KPIs) relevant to your objectives. KPIs may include website traffic, engagement rates on social media, conversion rates, and return on investment (ROI). This step lays the foundation for a structured evaluation.

Establishing Benchmarks and Goals

Set benchmarks based on historical data and industry standards. Define achievable goals aligned with your practice's growth objectives. Establishing clear benchmarks and goals provides a tangible framework for grading performance.

Grading Your Website Analytics

Analyzing Traffic Sources

Dive into your website analytics to scrutinize the sources of traffic. Assess the effectiveness of organic search, paid advertising, social media referrals, and direct traffic. Understanding where your audience originates empowers you to refine your acquisition strategies.

Evaluating User Behavior

Explore the user journey within your website. Assess the bounce rate, time spent on pages, and the most frequented sections. A positive user experience, reflected in favorable user behavior metrics, contributes to the overall success of your online presence.

Decoding Social Media Insights

Audience Engagement and Reach

Grade your social media performance by evaluating audience engagement and reach. Track likes, comments, shares, and overall visibility. A robust social media strategy not only attracts but also actively engages your audience.

Conversion Tracking

Explore the journey from social media interaction to conversion. Track the conversion rate of social media visitors into scheduled appointments or other desired actions. Data-driven insights from social media platforms guide strategic adaptations.

Assessing Advertising Platform Performance

ROI and Conversion Metrics

For those investing in advertising, assess the return on investment (ROI) and conversion metrics. Evaluate the cost per click (CPC), conversion rates, and the overall impact on practice growth. Data-driven decisions in advertising expenditure lead to optimized outcomes.

A/B Testing and Iterative Refinement

Embrace A/B testing methodologies to assess the effectiveness of different ad creatives, headlines, and targeting parameters. The iterative refinement based on A/B testing ensures that your advertising efforts evolve for maximum impact.

The Continuous Improvement Cycle

Cultivating a Culture of Continuous Improvement

Grading is not a one-time task; it's an ongoing process. Foster a culture of continuous improvement within your dental practice. Regularly revisit your benchmarks, reassess goals, and adapt strategies in response to evolving market dynamics.

Implementing Lessons Learned

Each data point tells a story. Implement lessons learned from your data analysis. If a particular strategy yields exceptional results, replicate and amplify it. Conversely, if an approach falls short, dissect the reasons and refine your tactics accordingly.

Realizing the Potential - A Success Story

A Data-Driven Transformation

Let's delve into a hypothetical success story, showcasing the transformative power of data-driven decision-making:

- Initial Analysis: Through meticulous data analysis, a dental practice identifies a decline in website traffic and engagement.

- Adaptation: Armed with insights, the practice adapts its content strategy, optimizing for search engines and addressing user preferences.

- Results: Subsequently, website traffic and engagement rates witness a significant uptick, leading to an increase in scheduled appointments and patient conversions.

Made in the USA
Middletown, DE
20 February 2024

49478714R00064